I am grateful to God for everything! And I believe that the meaning of life is to make sense of other lives.

Priscila Fineza
2024

This Book Belongs to:

○────────────────────────────────────○

P.N.F.©
all rights reserved

ALL RIGHTS RESERVED©
2024

No part of this publication may be reproduced, distributed, or transmitted in any form or by any means, including photocopying, recording, or other electronic or mechanical methods, without the prior written permission of the publisher, except for brief quotations incorporated in critical reviews and other specific noncommercial uses. Any unauthorized replica of this work is prohibited.

A.H.P.©
At Home publications

Test Color Page

Male Elephant

Female Alligator

Male Anteater

Female Anteater

Female Giraffe

Female Camel

www.ingramcontent.com/pod-product-compliance
Lightning Source LLC
Chambersburg PA
CBHW062117220526
45471CB00010B/3772